THE FLOATING CANDLES

THE FLOATING CANDLES

Poems by Sydney Lea

University of Illinois Press
Urbana Chicago London

2/1923
am. Lit.

...nk the editors of the following periodicals for permission
to reprint certain poems which first appeared (sometimes in
slightly different form) under their aegis:

Antaeus: "Toward Silhouette"
The Iowa Review: "To a Surgeon"
The New Republic: "A Natural Shame"
The Hudson Review: "Reaching Over," "At Hardscrabble,
Face to the Moon," "Trajectory"
Prairie Schooner: "Battle"
The Ohio Review: "There Should Have Been"
Connecticut Artists: "The Feud"
The Southern Review: "The One White Face in the Place"
The Seattle Review: "The Spherical Prism"
The Hollow Spring Review: "Sin and Fear"
"Accident," "The Floating Candles," and "Bernie's
Quick-Shave" originally appeared in *The New Yorker.*

Library of Congress Cataloging in Publication Data

Lea, Sydney, 1942–
  The floating candles.

  I. Title.
PS3562.E16F5   811'.54   82–2007
ISBN 0–252–00976–2 (cloth)   AACR2
ISBN 0–252–00977–0 (paper)

For my son and daughter, Creston and Erika,
and in memory of my brother Mahlon

It stood in our field
Big, old, and dirty it lies
The barn I played in

—*Creston Lea*

CONTENTS

DIRGE FOR MY BROTHER: DAWN TO DAWN

Why, like a sentence that qualifies itself
to forestall the inevitable period, did I want your dying
protracted? Till the fourth dawn it was. Then wisps
of red cloud striped the sky, white
stars achieved their anabasis into blue.
I told you all your life to face the real.
And you have seen it, eyelids blasted full
and black with it. Preliminary calls
of birds, mere echoes of the great bombed bubble
of your mind. The complete works. The death so obvious, early.

1 Moonman! Another dawn. Always for you
    a giant project. A stroke! Your awful explosion
    mocks my cautious sermon: Recognize
    Your Limits. You wouldn't till you had to. You,
    hawk-high above the world. So little
    comes, so little to listen for or see
    in elegy. Only reverberant will
    survives, and its blockaded ear, and eye.
    I stare at the stars to envy their height. They're fading.
    I hear pure bereavement rattle into the brain's

1

store: that region oddly military.
Moonman! Gung-ho commando! Your 'cycle shrieked
far out ahead of me. The gravel flew
like grapeshot out of a turn near Valley Forge.
You disappeared. I knew that barbed-wire fence
was strewn with you before I geared down, twice,
and rounded the bend where —like the wonder of
    planets—
you floated the horizontal a skyscape away.
Later you stopped a while (I hadn't caught you).
Your wild eyes rocketed over my preachments of calm.

2   O say can you see some order, brother? Mine
has been another day's distracting syntax.
The birds resign with evening. The world doesn't give
a hoot or whistle. Love and hate convolve,
are hard to conquer. I still cannot resist
the inclinations of sentence. I cast mine wide
into darkness. Superior, till it drove you half past crazy.
Earlier still, like a sniper you trained a gun
on me, hid in a bush at dusk. You screeched
at my dovish pleadings: "Stay on neutral ground!"
I recall the manic orders, remember clear as sirens

the gun and bush: Browning, Cardinalflower.
Within limits, my mind is clearer than ever. And yours?
For ninety-six hours a few poor straggling threads.
Artery, vein: blanched tatters of a flag,
of the mind that resisted internment. You flew at me quick,
drawing first blood with rock, shoe, stick. I waited
through the barrage, and generally so prevailed.
Yet Moonman! Your hand was open to others. A dog,
a child, the downcast. Always an easy touch.
I save some pictures of you, downtown. In one, your
    banner

2

fairly screams for THE END OF DISCRIMINATION
NOW! In another, you carry "Cherokee,"
that runaway on Chestnut Street, to drop her
at a preacher friend's: "Father, the girl's fourteen!"
Your mind could detect the rustle of city vultures
who'd swoop at her, but not —the preacher chuckles—
how her Jersey parents would wail when they discovered
their vagabond nestling nesting with Reverend Nigger.
The big twin coughed, exploded, and you lit out
—like a hawk, an eagle, Buck Rogers, Batman,
   Superman— Moonman!

down to that club (The Gilded Cage) where bluesmen
whined, "Don't the Moon Look Pretty, Shining Down
Through the Trees?" Then off again, soaring the asphalt,
tailpipes flaring like moon itself. It grinned
from crater to crater. In triumph, pleasure? Here lies
no mighty chief or leader as the world will measure
such a thing, and yet I feel the republic
stumble, crack. The mourners —the humble, rich,
the white and black— all look away. And I
among them. I, whose words should blast like twenty-one
   cannons. . . .

I. Out of Whiteness

*And those sublimer towers, the White Mountains of
New Hampshire, whence, in peculiar moods, comes that gigantic
ghostliness over the soul at the bare mention of that name. . . ?*
—Melville

1.   A Natural Shame

—for my mother

A NATURAL SHAME

The moon's small aura pins
the shadow of the sleeping children's
hobbyhorse down, black comic
monster, flat to the floor.
And I, inept at prayer,
clutching the bedclothes, I picture
wreck, gun, epidemic.
Tabloid headlines figure
in the elm tree's leaves.   Unmoored,
a shingle flaps into air.
Snapped from sleep so short
it only dried the throat
by a phrase: "A natural shame. . . ."
As if in her long career
nature had ever known shame —
this sentence, out of the country
junkyard that is the mind
untended, wakes me to sentry
duty. Unsettled by wind,
my old dog clicks along
the halls in disrepair.

Their ancestors' cells among
the bloodways of the babies
conspire, too soon, too soon.
The will would impose its stasis,
but in every pictured scene
I envision a moving thing:
bicycle tire spinning,
glucose bottle dripping
like heartbreak, murderer fleeing,
solid realist, Earth, unfurling
into romantic flight,
ink going white.

CHANTY: CLEANING THE RIVER-DRIVER

for Larry

In the dry town he drank
vanilla extract, tiny
bottles turning the barky
gums a hue of inland
myrtle. I shaved him Sunday
mornings, he shook and stank
and cursed (even me sometimes).
I'd studied Billy Grimes,
who'd scouted the logjams,
back straight up on the seat
of the boat. Stiff whiskers
resisting wind. One day
I dreamed we'd take to the river,
the sea-run salmons' beat
where he'd been a driver, plunge
paddles, skirting the half-sunk
deadheads, the eddies that strained them
till they sang in spume and sun.
Billy got happy-drunk.
Plunging the brush,
I worked the soapsuds in
those years, until inside

his sweat-stained union suit
he shrank. I grew on, saving
a picture while jetsam of glass,
beard and soap swelled wide
around the wicker armchair,
and chaw plugs, crushed
to a texture of peat or soot,
sank in the knotty cedar
of his cabin floor. I side-
stepped, cautious, wielding
the razor, child's eyes searching
the curious maplike lines
of Billy Grimes's face.
A rite that led all Lord's Days
back to a source, or end.
"I don't throw no bouquets,
you know, but you're a friend,
boy. . . . Fetch me another."
As he warmed and steadied, lather
sank like froth in sand.
The riverman's arms were good
where they met the foam-white shoulder.
The big thighs tensed when he stood,
and happy words made waves
of tendon in his neck, and flowed
into his eyes. He'd holler
at last, "Goddam, let's go
right off downriver, son.
The ocean! The Hundred Islands!
A month on every one!"
Then shambled out to the shade
where he dozed till after noon,
slumped against a tree,
though the wind —faint-scented with sea—
could cut you like a blade.

THERE SHOULD HAVE BEEN

With evening the groom and bride in groundfog
should have mounted the flatbed wagon, drawn
into the orchard by a vast dappled bullock.
Deer —tall stag, keen doe— should have come

so lacily gliding you'd have trouble to tell
their shapes apart from the onrushing mist.
An uncle was seated beside me. He held
white folds of my shirtcollar locked in a fist.

He rumbled: "My dancing days are all over,"
showing the blue stub under his knee
where skin like a windfall plum's was gathered.
I started. He gathered me back to see.

The buck's high rack would be velvet by rights,
would sparkle —I thought— with beads of the fog
in the firelight. Because there should have been firelight,
costume, concertina, song.

A wattled aunt secretly loosened a stay.
They could have been lovely, the bride and the groom,
waltzing together on pale tumbled blooms.
I thought how a falling star might display

the company's tears, good bubbles of wine,
the rings of emerald newts on the pond
in mating embrace. The close room was stained,
the hallways were humid, with beer and with rum.

The uncle insisted on hauling the needle
back to the same first groove, every dance.
He hummed a rough note under Ella Fitzgerald's
"Love for Sale." The party winced

at his crippled taste. Outside the rain
delivered howls from the turnpike, hammers,
drills, and curses of masons and carpenters
working all night on "Whispering Pines,

Half-Acre Estates" —they were "Coming Soon!"—
across the fields. My father started
the rust-pitted Chevy for home at one.
Leg propped on the seat, my uncle farted

and snored. My mother angled her nose
to the window. The asphalt wrinkled with steam.
There should have been some way of escape
for the lumpish opossum pair on the road,

dazed as the couple I'd saved from the cake,
jacked in their tracks by the onrushing beams.

AT HARDSCRABBLE, FACE TO THE MOON

27 August 1979

Seven years expire, and I return.
Barely spring then, small-leafed boughs now rich
with foliage pricked the moon hung full and perfect.
Someone had slapped a barn together here
a hundred years before. It sheltered me.
Nearby, a cellar hole so finely shimmed
its Yankee must have run plain out of time
or else ambition.   All is fallen.
Winters have so broken down the whole
affair I wonder if I've found the site.
Collapse has so transformed, uncentered it.

Face to the moon in the first fall night,
though it's still August. The moon has slimmed itself
down to a simple C, and histories
flit back like the last bloodsucking bugs of summer:

My mother, velvet-jacketed in bed,
is memory more smelled than recollected
by the eye —the fragrance of her sleep,
her hair washed out a night before. An hour

till terror —first fall day of school, my father
hums downstairs in time to perking coffee,
dark aroma rising through the cracks.
At school (old inn that crashed in '29)
there is a fireplace in the lobby with a motto:
Kindle Your Own Fire.
For me at eight years old, that stern inscription
might as well have been one Vergil showed
to Dante. Those first mornings I rehearse
whole drills of failure —balls that skitter past
my outstretched glove; a fumbled football; math;
disaster of a joke I try to tell
to two huge bullies, czars of a higher class.
In the bus I plug my ears and clench my eyes
to blank out history and face the blankness.
For even then I know how childish dread
can clothe the vanished days of summer recess
in falsity, and all their troubling signs:
the springhouse snapping turtle; smallmouth bass
clumped in a bucket with pondweed, cress, and slime.
These mornings odors mix before they fade:
the smell of turf where a bloodhorse runs and kicks
a trail of perfumed dew; the moist-sweet cow barn;
whiff of harshest soap and spanking linen,
uniforms of Irish chambermaids,
yet soon these virgins wear their small moustaches—
sweat of labor. Pearly, delicate.
The grooms put iodine on the broodmares' shanks
to toughen them with scar. The bullneck farmer
prowls the fields to shoot the hawk and crow.
In his sack a groundhog's head shows flies like stitches
around the fetid wounds. At last at dusk
the whirligig of sprinklers gathering night!

Night gathers, and I meddle with the embers
of my fire and shift to face the touring planet.

"Fly Me to the Moon." A snatch of song. . . .
I whirl her, Jeannie, all around the floor
as brassy saxophones appear to pour
a light on us. I dance like Fred Astaire,
I pray, because I'm sick almost to death
with love, and smirking in the corners stand
the older boys with car keys in their hands.
And hunkered in his wheelchair by the wall
sits crippled Jeremiah, with a flask.
He swears to beat the band. Tonight I think
he hurls his gob of curses —always meant
to bring a laugh— on me more desperately.
His street tough's parody —"I'll break your leg
and beat your goddam head with it!" —now seems
more full of gall and meaning than it's been.
Tonight I dream. I struggle with my crutches.
I chase a girl who shines on the leatherette
of a fleeing Buick. Laughter spills from the car.
I don't know if I wake to worse or better.
At worst I have the girl again with me.
At the wheel, my cousin (long since dead of drink).
His girlfriend, Barbie something, clings to him
as close as air. Ahead, far in the country,
Sonny's Modern Ballroom has Les Brown,
His Band of Renown, the rum we smuggle in.
Bleary-eyed above our later ring
of vomit, we all pledge unending love.

And here again I stir my ring of ashes,
humming brave and blind to will the present
closer, though the past has its own will.

The cellar hole was built with stones as fine
as Jeannie's ribs. My Jeannie, paunchy now.
The brook was lined with trout as big as bass
that stare up stinking from a memory
of buckets turned ideal in the sternness of time,
picturesque and ghostly as the ones
that lie among the weeds here on their own.
Winter was approaching, and the moon
was getting thin.

                    Now the moon approaches
the western rim, seems to balance there.

Camping in the barn, the woman curses
her man as he measures rock and levels wall,
half-crippled with his labor. Farm beasts ramble,
seeking food, neglected by this Yankee
bending to the present. Nothing but. . . .
She remembers linen, wine, soap, even Latin
learned in school: *amo, amas, amat.*
A brick-and-marble fireplace, summer dances. . . .
She recalls her giddy oath of steadfastness.
Her hair's a mat, her nightgown smeared with dregs
of rancid coffee.   Tonight is just tonight,
though she may wish to clench her eyes
or fix herself in blankness. The fire needs wood.

I rise in odorous night against my will
to gather sticks. My project is to face
the moon, yet I keep up a flame for now.
I go for windfalls in the pastures —ruined, full
of insects' counterpoint: *This was   This is*

TEMPTED BY THE CLASSICAL ON RETURNING FROM THE STORE AT TWENTY BELOW ZERO

Weather in place of God.
Legends of power in the store
float thick, misshapen as ghosts
around any Mather. The gilded
register quaintly gongs
among children devoted to sugar,
plastic. The walls are sweet
with rhetoric: TRY OUR OLDE
NEW HAMPSHIRE MAPLE SYRUP,
or angel-faced hippies' clichés
of redemption: Natural. Pure.
Pure nature hisses through nailholes:
the wind is "sharp as a knife,"
the snow "as tall as a steeple,"
the country "the last place God made."
Creosote clumps like sap
on the roof, outside. In idle
snowmobiles ("The Cat,"
"The Stinger") oil congeals.
Darkly. On television
a fool sings "You Light Up My Life."

Stuck to the truck's door handle,
wisps of heavy-fleshed thumb
come off to flitter from chrome
in the moon. The engine argues,
fires. The radio explodes
in the cab: Big Apple disco,
sex-electric. Barren
meadows glaze, untracked.
Hardwoods like frigid columns.
The floorboards are alabaster
with rime. Heart slows and whimpers,
set in a marbled coldness.
My memory's not what it was.
I paw at the dial to quiet
an ad: "Your Saving Place". . . .
Weak gratuitous beams
from my headlamps show a frieze:
two white coyotes turned to stone.
Perhaps there's some other salvation. . . .
The tarmac tells tonight
how easily it could brain
a man, despite the years,
Time's purchases, the lies:
the small stiff pile of condoms,
girls' blood, red as ideas
of summer, conversation
into the clogged telephone,
in which one offered his slogans —
"I love you," "I'm sorry"— or didn't,
the world of friendship's fetor,
the sprawling spring cotillions,
weddings, importunate children,
old folks in convalescent
"homes," fuel bills, cars.

I lose my words. Hard stars,
imperious, chip at my tumble
of hair, the dune of my skull,
embarrassing squalor of marrow
and meat. My fingers shoot
a spark of blue-near-silver.
In each myopic eye
a small moon settles and burns.
But I decline to brake
under the strait sharp sky.

TO A SURGEON

for R S

Nights, the stars
like polyps arrange
themselves in a body
I envision as world.
Or I say they hang
like clustered fates
waiting to fall
on the body, curses,
high pains that at last
will make us strange.

Your vision's straight
as razors, earned
each day gowned green,
your eye is schooled
and hands have learned
excision of trope.
Still in the theater,
I only seem
to unmask myself.
I borrow my terms

as I stretch this world
before you, body
and lumpish brain
and untrue dream
so often lashed
together by bloody
threads of figure,
like wildflowers sewn
in the stammering throat
of a brook, or muddy

lichens gathered
on the oaks' gnarled chests.
My children, exotic
and restless as cancer,
natter for breakfast.
Through frost-laced panes
I watch two hills
sag off the sun
and lust to be on them,
for the mind says *breasts*

though it knows that weather
has capped them with ice,
so slightly does world
conform to desire.
If hills are breasts,
how will we hide there
the winter-sick rabbits
thick as ward patients,
white, on the hillsides
waiting for death?

How account for the way
last autumn the flames
cauterized acres?
. . . The moon struggles up,
and the heart, that lame
redded hare, and woman
bloods to the moon.
The hills become beauty,
like health. A kestrel
rides the first beam

like the first pure thought
of the one who survived,
or a child who's swum
through amnios rank
as a new spring tide.
The metaphors clot
my conning of world's
immense operation,
and I'd lay myself open
for one hour, clarified,

malign or benign.
Sure eye, sure hand.
You shrug off my envy,
old sawbones plumbing
goiter and wen,
but you bend to the body
and worlds —moon, rabbit,
child, sun,
hawk, father,
high stars— attend.

ON BUZZARDS BAY, BETWEEN WORLDS

for Brendan Galvin

Ahead: will there be seawind? or any token
of weather, which seems to compensate
in part the solitude it makes —drift
of stars in the bay, dank summer
air that purges itself these nights,
the alewife run and waterfowl
navigating by moonlight.

Fleabane, beach plum lean to the cottages
inland from mullet-skipping coves
where schools of blues with their flint teeth cruise.
Autumn's dories yaw on their painters.
If the earthly house we live in goes
to wreck, will there be a house
not made with hands? He fingers

festoons of resin on pine.
The mundane mix of crunching gravel,
a shattered tumbler, laughter. Uproar
of greeting flutters the neighbors' shingles:

a boy —dark as weather-lashed timber—
supports an arriving girl. She shudders.
Lime chunks shrivel in expensive gin.

Like a squall a change is making. Tribes
of eels reconnoiter by dockside, snaky
clouds quick-slither across the Milky
Way in the blown high rooms of heaven.
Waves contradict themselves *click-click.*
Crabs bear their shelters away
over the jetty

like refugees. Our nature wastes,
says the minister down for the party.
We aren't at home in the body.
Random trails blink on the sandbar:
a dog snuffs a horseshoe husk in kelp
propped moonward.   Is there no vision
of ourselves as we are, the present ones?

He clings to the builded world,
though weed and shivered flotsam pool,
break up, and pool again —quicksilver.
Stone and mortar in the mind, he can't help it.
He puts one foot ahead of the other
as if he measured something
and progress were more than stroll.

Behind him: the nights of youthful erections,
elaborate plans!
Perhaps closer by than he thinks a whisper
rustles a hedge. The artifice
of the sun-browned boy, the repeated promise
that squeezes tears like greenwood pitch
from the girl. Wind bats at her gauzy dress.

Chilled, late August's insects fell,
fine noiseless rain on bay and ground,
vanished like carpenter ants in the playhouse
of childhood whose bite delivered him
into the body's text, the arms
of his father ringing
with the bell-smell of man.   A groaner

announces the groundswell under
the surface, checkered like tile.
Far out a rock dune looms —
awful cathedral, mist
laying slabs around it: headstones. Landward
the joy contrived in the cedar summer
place collapses, the lighthouse beacon

gutters as fog sifts down like ruin.
Distance calls, repels,
statelier haunted mansion of later
childhood, now to be entered or not.
A skiff on the beach. He may row
—shoulder and back in their architecture
making bold statement— or not.

BERNIE'S QUICK-SHAVE (1968)

for Paul Mochary

At dawn three shearsmen
dress in white, exact
non-shade of the blank
prospect that they'll encounter
but —out of their courage—
they refuse to acknowledge.
Or is it their impotence?
Out on the Green,
which in this February
is more in fact
a White, long-haired
students from the college
return to their monuments of ice:
the carnival theme
this winter is *Life
in the Future.* Machines
in this fantastic tableau
are conceived to replace
all dulling labor.
The students in arrogance
consider *themselves* the Future.
Sad, the way

that Frank, Ed, Mike
—pale monoliths,
three plinths
behind the pane— all day
will regard these children in beards
and tattered pants
as the Future, too:
a season gone away
before its own arrival.
The chair keeps yawning like
a dead man's abandoned
recliner. The lather won't rise
to match the drifts
and windrows by their trailers.
It remains the latent billow
within their minds,
as fog and whitecap waves
become mere thought in sailors
grounded —vague things
to fill the void they prophesy
as yet another night
falls on the village
shops, forlorn and white
as those few unconsoling early stars.

At length, berobed,
they struggle to their cars,
whose windshields seem at first
to cloud with steam.
Their radios often bear them
news of former
clients now, last regulars

turned in this decade hairless
or thinly crowned with slow-
grown locks that shiver
in the frigid estate to which
their whiteness is witness. . . .
The radios announce
old shavers gone,
like figures one has met
within a dream
or landscapes that will never
be replenished.
Snow drifts down like talcum.
But tomorrow dawn
they'll stand again,
tragic as winter gravestones,
those for whom some central thing has vanished.

2. The Feud

THE FEUD

I don't know your stories. This one here
is the meanest one *I've* got or ever hope to.
Less than a year ago. Last of November,
but hot by God! I saw the Walker gang,

lugging a little buck. (A sandwich size.
It *would* be. That bunch doesn't have the patience.
I'd passed up two no smaller, and in the end
the family had no venison that fall.)

I waved to them from the porch —they just looked up—
and turned away. I try to keep good terms
with everyone, but with a crowd like that
I don't do any more than necessary.

It wasn't too much cooler back inside.
A note from my wife on the table said the heat
had driven her and the kids to the town pond beach
to sit. That made some sense. It's the last that will.

I peeked out quick through the window as the Walkers'
truck ripped past, and said out loud, "Damn fools!"
The old man, "Sanitary Jim" they call him,
at the wheel, the rifles piled between

him and "Step-and-a-Half," the crippled son.
In back, all smiles and sucking down his beer,
"Short Jim" and the deer. Now Short Jim seems all right.
To see his eyes, in fact, you'd call him shy.

He doesn't talk quite plain. Each word sounds like
a noise you'd hear from under shallow water.
I didn't give it too much thought till later,
when the wife and kids came home, and wanted to know

what in Jesus' name that awful smell was,
over the road? Turns out that Walker crew
had left their deer guts cooking in the sun.
And wasn't that just like them? Swear to God,

to leave that mess beside a neighbor's house
for stink, and for his dogs to gobble up?
And there was one thing more that puzzled me:
why wouldn't they take home that pile of guts

to feed *their* dogs? A worthless bunch —
the dogs, I mean, as well as them. You'd think
they wouldn't be above it. Every decent
dog they ever had was bullshit luck,

since every one they run is one they stole
or mooched out of the pound. You'll see them all,
hitched to one lone post, dung to the elbows,
and every time they get themselves a new one,

he'll have to fight it out until the others
either chew him up or give him up.
I guessed I'd do this feeding for them, so
I raked up all the lights into a bag

and after nightfall strewed them in their dooryard
with a note: "Since I'm not eating any deer meat,
I'd just as quick your guts rot somewhere else
as by my house." And signed my actual name.

The whole thing's clear as Judgment in my mind:
the sky was orange, the air so thick it burned
a man out of his senses. I'm the one.
And evening never seemed to cool me off,

though I'm a man whose aim is not to truck
in such a thing. I've lost most of my churching,
but don't believe in taking up with feuds.
I usually let the Good Lord have His vengeance.

Nothing any good has ever grown
out of revenge. So I was told in school
when I slapped up Lemmie Watson, because he broke
the little mill I built down on the brook.

And so I learned. I spent the afternoons
that week indoors, and I've been different since,
till this one day. Then something else took over.
There passed a week: they stove my mailbox up.

At least I don't know who in hell beside them
would have done it. I had a spare. (The Lord
knows why.) I cut a post and put it up,
and could have left the blessed fracas there,

and would have, as my wife advised me to.
And I agreed. I told myself all night,
my eyes wide open, lying there and chewing,
"Let it go." And would have, as I claim,

but two days passed, and they came hunting coons
on this side of the ridge. I heard their hounds.
(God knows what *they* were running. Hedgehogs? Skunks?
It could have been.) Out on the porch

I heard *tick-tick.* Dog paws, and all my dogs
began to yap and whine. I made a light.
Shaky, thin as Satan, a docktail bitch,
a black-and-tan (almost), was looking in.

I made of her. She followed me as if
I'd owned her all my life out to the kennel.
I stuck her in the empty run that was
Old Joe's before I had to put him down.

I filled a dish with meal. She was a wolf!
The first square feed she'd had in quite a time.
My wife kept asking what I could be up to.
Likes to worry. Next day I drove clear

to Axtonbury, to the county pound.
"This dog's been hanging round my house all week.
Don't know who she belongs to." Lies, of course.
I had her collar locked in the Chevy's glovebox.

I wouldn't harm a dog unless I had to,
and figured this one stood a better show
to make out at the pound than at the Walkers'.
But the Walkers didn't know that. Driving home,

I flung the collar in their dooryard. After dark,
and spitting snow, six inches by next day,
late in December now, toward Christmas time.
Things shifted into higher gear despite me.

Or on account of me. Why not be honest?
I know that nowadays it's not the fashion
to think a person's born what he becomes;
but Sanitary Jim, his wife and family:

I never gave it too much thought but must
have figured right along that they belonged
to that great crowd of folks who *don't* belong.
Their children wear their marks right on them: speech

you hardly understand, a rock and sway
where a normal boy would take an easy stride.
And in and out of jail. If they can't find
another bunch to fight with, why, they'll fight

with one another. (Sleep with one another
too, if talk can be believed. Somehow
two homely sisters are in the mix as well.)
Short Jim beat an uncle or a cousin

—I disremember— beat him right to death.
(It's not the fashion either nowadays
to keep a violent man in jail. A month, no more,
goes by, and Short Jim's on the town again.)

But back to what I just began. The Walkers
are as bad as banty roosters, and I figured
they were meant somehow to be. Where most of us
are meant to eat one little peck of dirt,

they eat a truckload. Is it any wonder,
then, I didn't make a special point
of mixing with them? No more than I would
with any crowd that filthed itself that way.

But mix with them I did. It seemed as if
their style of working things reached up and grabbed me.
I was in the game so quick it turned my head.
The snow came on, the first big storm of winter,

that night I pulled the trick with the docktail's collar.
In the morning, barely filled, I saw their tracks
around my kennel. But *my* runs both are solid
chain-link, and the doors are padlocked shut.

They mean a thing or two to me, those dogs.
I keep the keys right on me. No one else
—no family, no good friend— can spring a dog
of mine. That way, I know they're there, or *with* me.

I'm only puzzled that they never growled. They do
as a rule. I was surely glad the Walkers hadn't
had the sense to bring along some poison.
A dog's a dog, which means he's five-eighths stomach.

Thinking on this gave me bad ideas.
But I'll get to that when time is right. For now,
I called myself a lucky fool, out loud,
and bolted both dogs shut inside their houses

nights. I judged this thing would soon blow over.
I burned a yardlight too, which I'd never done.
And that (I guessed) was the last they'd come past dark.
You know, the funny part of this whole battle

up to now, when you consider who
I'd got myself involved with, was that neither
side had come right out into the open.
The only thing I knew for sure they'd done

was leave a mess of guts out on my lawn.
The only thing for sure they knew of me —
that I returned that mess to its right home.
The mailbox and the collar and the tracks. . . .

For all we either knew, the Boss was making
visions in our eyes which, feeling righteous,
we took upon our *selves* to figure out.
And since, between the parties, I guessed *I*

had better claim to righteousness than they did,
I'm the one that —thinking back— began
to read the signs according to my will.
How many times have village hoodlums stove

a mailbox up? Or just plain village kids?
How many times, to mention what comes next,
has one old drunk shitkicker or another
raised some hell outside Ray Lawson's Auction

and Commission Sales on Friday night? And still,
I judged it was the Walkers who had slashed
all four of my new pickup's summer tires.
(Four months had passed.) And judged it quick as God.

The pickup spraddled like a hog on ice. It cost me
two hundred dollars just to run it home.
Next day I passed Short Jim as he came out
of Brandon's store and sized him up, and looked

at him: a man who'd killed another man,
but shyness in his eyes. He looked away.
And if I'd looked away just then. . . . Instead,
I saw a basket full of winter apples,

Baldwins mostly, full of slush and holes.
No wonder Brandon had that crop on sale!
Four cents each was asking more than enough
for winter apples still unsold in April.

If the top one hadn't had a hole as big,
almost, as half a dollar. . . . By God, where
would we be now? But there it was, the hole,
and I got notions. Maybe fate is notions

that you might have left alone, but took instead.
I did. I bought that apple, and another
just for show. And a box of pellets, too —
more rat pellets than I ever needed,

more than I could stuff into that hole
and still have stay enough in the rotten skin
to hold them in enough to fool a hog
that he *had* an apple. Walkers' hog, I mean.

They penned her on the far side of the road
from where that firetrap shack of theirs was built.
I didn't set right out. That apple sat
as much as seven days up on a post

of metal in the shed, where even rats
—Lord! let alone my kids— could never reach it.
And it sat inside my mind. Especially nights.
Or say it burned, the while I cooled myself

—or tried to do, with every nerve and muscle—
in bed, and said the same thing over and over:
"Nothing good will ever grow from feuds."
And just to get the apple *out* of mind,

spoke such damn foolishness you never heard:
"Old Mother Hubbard," "Stars and Stripes Forever"
(tried to get the words of one to go
along with the rhymes and rhythms of the other).

Then went down that seventh night, as if it was
another person who was going down
inside the shed (because the person I
believed I was kept up the sermon: "Nothing

any good from any feud," and so on),
picked the apple down, and put it in
my pocket, and —the moon was full— began
the uphill climb across the ridge. To Walkers'.

Stopped for breath at height of land, I turned
to see the house, where everyone was sleeping,
wondered what they dreamed, and if their dreams
were wild as mine become when moon's like that —

they say there's nothing in it, but as God
will witness me, a full moon fills my head,
asleep or not, with every bad idea.
One spring, the moon that big, a skunk came calling

in the shed, and my fool tomcat gave a rush.
The smell was worse than death. It woke me up,
if I was sleeping (I'd been trying to),
and till the dawn arrived, for hours I felt

the stink was like a judgment: every sin
from when I was a child till then flew back
and played itself again before my eyes.
High on the ridge, I felt I might reach out

and touch that moon, it was so close, but felt
that if I reached it, somehow it would burn.
It was a copper color, almost orange,
like a fire that's just beginning to take hold.

Your mind plays tricks. You live a certain while
and all the spooky stories that you read
or hear become a part of memory,
and you can't help it, grown or not, sometimes

the damnedest foolishness can haunt you. Owls,
for instance. I know owls. How many nights
do they take up outside, and I don't think
a thing about it? *That* night, though,

a pair began close by me. I'd have run,
the Devil take me, if the light had been
just one shade brighter, I'd have run right home
to get out of the woods or else to guard

the house, the wife, the kids. I don't know which.
A rat or mouse would shuffle in the leaves
and I would circle twenty yards around it.
I was close to lost until I found the brook

and waded it on down. It was half past two.
The moon kept working higher till I saw
the hog shed just across the road from Walkers' house.
There wasn't that much difference in the two.

I'm a man can't stand a mess. But they,
the boys and Sanitary Jim. . . . Well, they
can stand it. Seems that that's the way
that they *prefer* it. That hovel for the pig

was made of cardboard, chimney pipe, and wanes.
They'd driven I don't know how many sections
of ladder, side by side, into the mud
for fencing. Come the thaw each year, the ground

will heave that ladder up, and then you'll find
a pig in someone's parsnips. Anyway,
I looked the matter over, and the worry
that I'd felt about the thing that I was doing —

well, it went away. I felt as pure
as any saint or choirboy hunkered there.
I crept up on my knees and clapped the gate
(a box spring from a kid's bed) so the pig

would have a peek. I don't know why, exactly,
but I felt like watching as she took the apple
from my hand. It wouldn't do to leave it.
She just inhaled it, didn't even chew.

I backed up to the brook and watched some more,
then stepped in quick, because that poison sow
began to blow and hoot just like a bear.
The job was done. I hadn't left a track.

I don't know just what you'll make of this:
I fairly marched back up across the ridge
as if I made that climb four times a day.
The air was cold and sweet and clear, the way

it is when you can see the moon so plain.
I walked on to a beat and sang the hymns
—or sang them to myself— I'd got by heart
so many years before: "Old Rugged Cross"

and "Onward Christian Soldiers" and "Amazing
Grace," and never noticed how the cold
had numbed my feet till I was back in bed.
No one woke up. I slept two righteous hours.

You jump into a feud, and every trick's
like one more piece of kindling on the fire.
That's how I think of it, and you'll see why.
Come evening of the next day, I was sick.

You don't go paddling nighttimes in a brook
in April, and expect it's just a trick.
All night it felt like someone had a flatiron
and kept laying it between my shoulder blades.

My feet and legs were colored like old ashes.
My throat was sore enough I couldn't speak.
My wife, who didn't have a small idea
of where I'd been beside beneath the quilts,

lay it all to how I carried on.
"You've heard the old expression, 'sick with worry.'
That's what you've brought yourself, I think, from scheming
on those godforsaken Walkers." She was right,

but not the way she thought she was. In time,
there wasn't any use, I had to go
down to the clinic, twenty miles away.
You know those places: wait there half a day,

then let them pound you, scratch their heads, and scratch
some foolishness on a scrap of paper, wait
the other half while the druggist dubs around
to find the thing he's after. Come home poor.

If it was only poor that I came home!
I drove through town at fifteen miles an hour.
Swear to God I couldn't wheel it faster,
the way I was. It was a job to push

the throttle down, and I could scarcely see,
so blinked my eyes a time or two when I reached
the flat out by the pond. Above the ridge
the sky was copper-orange, and thick black smoke

was flying up to heaven, straight as string.
I thought I felt the heat. (But that was fever.)
By Jesus, that was my house. "Chimney fire,"
I said out loud, or loud as I could talk,

my throat ached so. The words were just a whisper,
and they sounded wrong the minute they came out.
I felt like I would die from all this sickness.
They called me "walking wounded" at the clinic:

pneumonia, but just barely, in one lung;
but now I felt my blood would burst the skin
and I'd just up and die inside that truck.
I squinched my eyes and lay the throttle on.

I meant to do some good before I died.
My wife was wrestling with a metal ladder
that had sat outside all winter, though I'd meant
to get it under cover every day.

I used it cleaning chimneys. It was stuck
in puddle ice beside the western wall.
I jumped out of the truck before it stopped,
and fell, and got back up, sweet Christ,

I tried to run, and every step I took
was like a step you take in dreams, the space
from road to house seemed fifteen thousand miles.
I stumbled to the shed and grabbed an ax

and put it to the ground to free the ladder,
but the ground just wouldn't give the damned thing up,
and every lick was like I swung the ax
from under water. I had no more force

than a kid or cripple. My kid, meanwhile, cried
from behind a big storm window, "Daddy? Daddy?"
It sounded like a question. I gave up
and tried to call back up to him. I couldn't.

My words were nothing more than little squeaks,
and when they did come out, they were not plain.
And so my wife began to call the boy,
"Throw something through the window and jump out!"

He threw a model boat, a book, a drumstick.
He couldn't make a crack. I flung the ax.
It missed by half a mile. I threw again
and broke a hole, and scared the boy back in.

That was the last I saw him. Like a woman
sighing, that old house huffed once and fell.
Out back, beside the kennel, our baby daughter
danced and giggled to hear the howling dogs.

I went into dead faint. And Hell could come
for all of me. And that is what has come.
Thirty years gone by since Lemmie Watson
broke my little mill of sticks and weeds

down by the brook, and I kicked the tar from him
and stayed indoors all week when school let out.
And Mrs. What's-Her-Name, I disremember,
fussing at her desk, would shake her head

and ask out loud if one small paddle wheel
was worth all this? I had to answer No.
I had to write it down, "No good can grow
from any feud." I wrote it fifty times

each afternoon. And then one afternoon
the Walker crew lay down a string of guts
across the road. . . . The part of life you think
you've got done living lies in wait like Satan.

For me, it was revenge. And what to do
right now? The house is gone, the boy, and I
believe I know just how they came to be.
But do I? Do I know what led to what

or who's to blame? This time I'll let it go.
No man can find revenge for a thing like this.
They say revenge is something for the Lord.
And let Him have it. Him, such as He is.

3.   *Fact. Or Sublime*

THE ONE WHITE FACE IN THE PLACE

So often true back then,
that platitude,
when in Harlem   Baltimore
north Philly   D.C.
I wasn't altogether
unwelcome in the blues
joints. I'd travel across
two states to see
the shuck-and-jive of Muddy
Waters' band,
the great Ray Charles, for whom
I'd travel farther,
the Lightnings (Slim and Hopkins),
Bobby Bland,
some wonderful unfamous
wreck named Arthur. . . .

Ray would cry out "Drown
in My Own Tears"
with that heartbreak keyboard tinkle
before the refrain.
Here in whitest New Hampshire

fifteen years
later, and seven states
away, the tin roof tinkles
with new rain
after a morning of purest
New England blue.
I walked the high-country beat,
for reminiscence. . . .
"Everybody understands
them mean old blues!"
So Ray would shout. And then
as now, I sensed
that I might be included.
Right or wrong.

Today in the woods, the one
white face in the place,
I marveled that all that pain
could turn to song!
The testament of will. . . .
Just as out of their innards
the spiders' lace
had strung itself from every
bush and tree:
makings. And yet I thought,
high on the hill,
how —if indeed it's a fact
that on every acre there are
a million of these
deft spinners— then I was a million-
fold trailed and tracked,
attacked, fished for, observed,
climbed upon,
and caressed by design and brilliance.

What end do they serve?
One true fact is that
the one white
face in the place became
ever more overgrown
with the spiders' snares. I fought
through them as I fight
through many reminders. Reminders,
though, of what?
Well, maybe ambivalence if not
plain contradiction.
The webs are a sign of welcome
and malediction,
if spiders speak from their guts.
Yet, in another age,
these thready secretions
were regarded as stuff with which
to stanch a wound. . . .

It's as if what's ripped from us
becomes the thing that heals.
The blues: to understand them
is to be confounded.
Just so, walking such country,
Emerson feels
that "nothing is got for nothing."
I, the stranger,
understood —if I did—
the blues because
I *was* the stranger, at ease
because of the danger:
white boy in the dark
after the Blue Laws'
curfew amid the forbidden

tastes and odors
of gin, sweat, pomade
and Mary Jane.
And more overpowering than these
—hotter, harder—
that sense which comes again
with returning rain,
which blackens the world in order
to dress it in lightning
and drowns the fields in quiet
that they may speak
with the murmuring voice of a million
ancient waters;

that sense of a ray of hope
from out of the frightening
wreckage, and a thread of despair
from out of the bland
spun repetitions of handsome
brightblue days;
and from platitudinous matter
the makings of grand
structure, beauty, which are random
reminders still.

Dark blood pulses in the one
white face in the place
and will.

TRAJECTORY

for M R B

Implausible flight, flotation
of a Dodge Ram pickup truck above
the interstate, Montreal-bound.
How could it be? Slow, revolutionary,
drifting just above
blown snow, below the stars
dipping with winter near road level. In such suspense,
which surely lasts
no longer than a second, life
rewinds.
          Yet we aren't there, my love.
"Not there," we tell ourselves,
each in his silent voice, or hers. Not poised
in aching distance, far from what just passed,
just yesterday
—the dances and initial kisses
light as flakes at zero—
and nearer to
what transpires at last.
No, not. We are
preserved from ending, although it's late
to urge some caution

on the driver, fool who dreamed himself
immune from nature's mocking of our transit.
The road's slick grin turned mean
and spit between its teeth and tossed him,
truck and all, into mild trajectory
till he landed. Flight itself was lovely:
the steel cab caught the pure description
of planets on its panels as they circuited
before our very eyes. The crash was dull
and disappointing, although we're not
mere gawkers anxious for titillation.
Did we stop to help? Or did we
dream those figures
dead in noncommittal repose?
Let disaster come. Let it, though, arrive
with dramatic flare and impact,
we say, wishing them in fact
upon ourselves, hours later,
sidereal time set back in motion, our cheap hotel
bed crackling like a frozen rut
and each locked up in his
or her compartment of mute desire
transcending flesh.
                    Man and woman in a cab, they sped
together north, as we have. We imagine
them like us, but with greater lust —
minds trained on the coming
white explosion
of the city above the tedious plateau
of upper Vermont, Gallic palaver,
adolescent bodily thrill. Their end was more
and less. We wonder,
did words pass between them, cruising
above ironic ground? Did words

pass between *us* in that arrested moment?
Neither one remembers,
but what might we have spoken? Peculiar oaths
we cry out as in its soaring sex
peaks before
the hurtling back to earth?
Strange callings on a Savior,
as if that spirit could protract
the trip we started so far back
in bodies that were so light
that innocence occurs to us
—here, later—
almost as disembodiment
and life back then as endless flight.

REACHING OVER

the death of Jimmy K

This time will be the crossing.
This time it's not as if
he hasn't reached for a match
and touched his cigarette and —mooning—
put it back in the box still glowing.
Not as if he hasn't gone
upstairs with the jug in one hand,
the other clapping the rail,
or as if the small bomb of brimstone
has not lit the others and grown,
if only enough to reach
the fuse of shelf paper trailing
from the hooch-soaked cupboard above
like the single sad strand of a smirched
bandage to the can of Sterno perched
in waiting to sigh into flame
—blue eye in a dark recess—
or the cupboard itself doesn't glow
and reach the same faint blue in time.
He might have studied the quickening climb
through the spectrum that followed, the change
from blue to green to yellow

to orange, like the sun's at prime.
Upstairs he lies in bed between dream
and whatever life is. It's not as though
he hasn't an eye, doesn't know
the way disaster can reach
to a kind of splendor —glow
of the world in its own undoing. Below,
bottles pop like lamp bulbs, fuel
the process. Not that you wouldn't
hear or smell the charring.
But each mirage overrules
the instinct to flight: each horse he's schooled
high-jumps in a paddock, all ribbons and plaits,
a lake in Ontario lies
clear to the shining bottom,
that only an otter obfuscates,
marking the slick with a razor-fine wake,
a martin glows in a tree,
an eagle patrols a shelf
as the desert explodes into light,
the guide in his galabia grunts —poetry!—
and a prow cuts a full blue sea.
Not that he's wrong. At last
the drink will carry him over.
It's not that he hasn't reached
over, or fire hasn't found its path
this time. He has, it has.

ACCIDENT

Never to remember
New York City
Mingus's splendid tirades
Chico Max
the MJQ or early Gerry
He rides
His bike shooting out of woods like a switchblade
Onto the lane
In our meadow where night air
Leaves a slick on the gravel. This dawn
Has no steam breathing through pavement cobbles
But a purple moth struggles
With the wet burden like Elvin
Jones in a gin-soaked club
And with his half-shucked shell
Into such brief improvisation
Of beauty that if the boy were nearer
Or it were an hour later
(Daytime frogs on the beat
Like morning cops —Ninth at Broadway, dawn,
Twenty years gone—
Or my daughter doing her scat

Voices drowning
The riff of wings like tiny high-hat cymbals)
I would never have noticed

The muted sun like Miles cuts through
The mistflumes' chorus
On the river where mayflies
Lose their shifting hold on pebbles
At the bottom and make their way up
And trout at their stations hover like trebles
In the haysweet hills
The I I think I am
Beats against the snare of the past
And sleep and dream
Hard case
My son repeats
The terrible solo again
And again in his seventh summer
That decrescendo
Dreaming his bike a flyer
Set for the moon like Diz
Last night my baby daughter
Poked a thumb at the ofay moon
And sang, "I want it." She thinks
It's Big Rock Candy. Meatfat and drink
Clash in my sour intestines
Like Monk's odd clusters in the old Half Note
The moth flies up
And clings in splendor to a screen

Hanging in country air
There's the boy's high wail
As his fender shivers like a tambourine

BATTLE

After George Bellows's "Both Members of This Club"

A lie of course, a lie accommodating
the time's loose law. Each fighter was
elected for the night —night of The Battle—
hurrahed or hissed, and then sent packing.
In the bottom quarter of the canvas, actual
members' faces, in death's-head grins and leers.
The colored boxer's face can't be distinguished
from the upper quarter's background of solid black.
The white boy wears a bloody makeup beard,
but it isn't makeup, is it? Their wrists seem soldered,
and the members' merry eyes suggest some joke,
as if a brass band's oom-pah beat were pulsing
and in parodic outrage both the boxers,
done with trading punches, had started waltzing.
But see the high-volt tension in the ropes,
the knees that flex so tight you'd think the caps
would burst the skin, and pectoral muscles show
the evening's fierceness.   So does the sad
contemplative look of a cornerman who grasps
some turn in the bout he doesn't like the look of.

We look, but can't determine what it is.
We say of the two, They are above it —gods.
We say, The ignorant lookers-on will sizzle
in hell, and that the painter knew it all.
Or that these Battlers both are made of oil
and water on a canvas —fabrications
accommodating a set of aesthetic laws.
Yet somewhere now an actual toilet bowl
stands ready to take the kidneys' ring of blood,
real blood, for somewhere there's a canvas
flecked with the actual colors of election.
This isn't that rose gore of old Romance.
The loser's eyes turn inward to the blackness.
The winner's eyes turn upward to the blackness.
We look, and say, The Battle is a dance.

.

RANKING THE HARDWOODS

for Harry Schultz, retiring from college teaching

I've lumbered through the musty
woods of trope for this, dear Harry,
searching some new figure. Failing,
lapsed in loss,
I lean upon the tale-worn trusty Oak,
the straight, the tough.
Yet we both know one could
do worse than end up lost in woods
when words fail.
                    Woods can also fail,
of course. The sappy Maple,
just for instance, made
into a staff, will check and warp.
The Aspen quivers, sensitive
to every wind. Try it in heat,
it shows its deeper nature,
softness, froth and steam.
The Leverwood, or Hornbeam,
shows its muscle, but its skin
peels off like onion hide.
It's now one tree and now another.
The Basswood leaf's a giant heart,

60

but it's a trying tree to know in winter,
so various its bark.
As analog, it can't be true
enough for you.
The Hardhack's not a tree at all,
a pesky whip, a bother,
grown when grander forest fails
or burns. Great crops of it.
They lean against you,
with the season,
and can't take fire.
Beneath its smooth exterior,
the Beech is gnarled and twisted.
Kindle the Paper Birch or Ash,
but seek no lasting coals.
The Thorn Plum stabs you from its thicket.

The Oak endures at height of land,
sending its rugged runners downward.
No valley child remembers other
than Oak for climbing from soil to crownward.
Oak will make a door secure
against impertinence. It makes
as well a door plumb, square and sure
to open in all weathers.
Oak for beams. Good Oak to hold
spring water, holy as men's tears.

Some violence —hatchet, saw, or storm—
may cleave the Oak. Still it appears,
inside as outside, clear and bold.
No better wood for staying warm.

(29 May 1979)

DEAD OF WINTER, ECHO, DAUGHTER

in praise of women, especially Erika

Having spent the anxious early hours
of morning confronting
the white of paper,
which seems unchanging, I lift
my daughter —that presence,
however tiny, that makes me
better.   The still
photos on my study sill make
a male morgue: that's just
how it's fallen out, dead father,
brother, teachers,
friends —all men. Desiring
some reiteration, I
rush back to my desk each dawn, or mount
the same old trail
above my house. Each winter I fight
the same two pipes that freeze
whenever the weather plunges.
I hide my gratitude
for these rites, small secrets —such as they are—
that anneal one year to another.
Outside, the girl, lightly astride

my shoulders, improvises chatter
in the nimbi of breath I puff,
which turn to crystal and settle
on her hood's bogus wool ruff.
I fear my own
and the mean day's ice will make her
frigid. But she is sturdy,
merry, desiring everything new,

all that our climb can provide.
I think of the father, brother,

and raging young chums of boyhood
and rising manhood
gone into whiteness. Despite
apparent heat, how cold
we were to one another!
Secretive, never unguarded,
unlike this child, none
of whose thoughts or words has a guard,
though I cling to her
body for very life. If she falls
it will be in spite of me.
Her button of sex
seems to thaw my neck, and I try
to turn toward her.
She tells me my hands are soft
and warm, but here
in the world so many unjust
men keep carrying on. And why
are we hard? Of all men, I
ought to know. Or so
I tell myself in characteristic lust
to prevail, even as breath

gets short, and behind me
weather scatters
what scribbles have marked my trail
in snow. I bellow
through every crack
in wind —puny self-
advertisement that brings an echo.
My daughter laughs,
wise ingenue.
She sees the humor in how,
when I shout at the sky,
the sky shouts back.

THE SPHERICAL PRISM

From a snip of nylon fishing leader,
it's suspended in the picture window through which
these years I've watched fall down
rain, snow, sleet
and fog —my element this morning:
how can I see outside
the prism itself? On whose glass in flattened light
the fingerprints of my children reveal themselves.
I will not wash them off
nor think of replacing
that wisp from which the small sphere hangs. In artificial
weather of my house, it could be any month,
and seasonal themes —determined as I
appear to myself at times— blank out. Despair
or liberation? I think of the brave imprisoned
who gather tropes of hope from their forced regard
of rat or spider; of the ash-colored kid
in the slum who is bound
to prevail, conning
a serious book; of self-sustaining
winter beavers denned
in musk and murk. Unable to lift my eyes

to the hills, I wonder from what I'll cull
a little life, hoarding my threads of rhetorical sadness.

There rises in mind a shape:
my son at five, awkwardly poised on the sill,
determined to reach the prism as daylight
breaks the horizon's rim in world-rotation
until he can spin it, make it burst with jewels.
And my daughter, wailing to be raised,
or to have the future, that she may make
the thing revolve
on its fragile axis —the leader that I am
drawing by habit out of the partial dark of recall. . . .

I cut it from the line that day on the pond
when the heavy buck in velvet burst from the east
shore and swam to the west. I snarled my gear in reaction,
beyond any ready repair. I waited to see what drove him,
seeking always a history. But there was nothing,
only his impulse to go, break bounds. I stayed.
I studied the hole
in woods from which he had leapt. Though sun now laid
a foot on Mousley Mountain, and evening was coming,
I stayed and marked the tattered mosses, failed will to prevail
of sapling whips that the buck had raked with his horns,
playing at preparation. Now I recall
till I almost see them the spectral hues
on the fish in the boat to which I turned my eyes,
and how I turned my thoughts from them to remembered
colors of cloud, rain, snow. Till sun was lost.

How long before it lights the prospect again?
I've been a slave to reflection in this long morning,
and in this lifetime. I'm determined on revolution —

to fact, but not to fact as figure locked
in the dim of what has vanished. And I am bound
to cut away the lure of self-pity, language
and theme to which by a thread I hold like pearls.
I will reach toward that object, training my eyes
on the many facets, as if —though fog persists—
they light upon my walls patterns distinct and varied
as children, my children, squalling at play,
troutspots, vigorous beasts.
As if the sun will return if the prism is whirled.

THE FLOATING CANDLES

for my brother Mahlon (1944–80)

You lit a firebrand:
old pine was best.
It lasted, the black
pitch fume cast odors
that, kindling a campfire
or such, today
can bring tears. You held
the torch to one dwarf
candle stub then another
and others till each
greased cup filled up
and the stiff wicks stood.
Ten minutes a candle,
but we were young
and minutes seemed long
as the whole vacation.
We chafed and quarreled.
The colors bled
like hues in jewels.
At last we carried
a tub of the things
down the path to the Swamp

Creek pond through seed-
heavy meadows where katydids
whined like wires
in mid-August air's
dense atmosphere.
An hour before bedtime.
Reluctant grownups
would trail behind,
bearing downhill
the same dull patter
and cups brimful
of rye, which they balanced
with the same rapt care
that balanced our load.
The bullfrogs twanged
till you touched a wick
with the stick, still flaming,
then quieted. We heard them
plop in the shallows,
deferring to fire,
and heard in the muck
turtles coasting in flight.
The night brought on
a small breeze to clear
the day that all day
had oppressed us, to dry
the sweat that our purposeful
hour had made,
to spread the glims
like dreamboats of glory
in invisible current.
That slow tug drew
the glowing flotilla
south to the dam.

The bank brush —hung
with gemmy bugs— shone
and made great shadows
as the candles slipped by,
erasing the banal
fat stars from the surface.
This was, you could say,
an early glimpse
of a later aesthetic.
Nonsense. We know
it was cruder than that
and profounder, far.
It showed us the way
the splendid can flare
despite the flow
of the common. Now,
despite the persistence
of heat and quarrel,
the thickness of wives
and children and time,
such shinings on water
are fact. Or sublime.

II. Ghost Signs, Seasons, Earth and Air

Reflections on the Hunt

The mission of thought is to construct archetypes;
I mean to point out from among the infinite figures
that reality presents those in which, because of their
greater purity, that reality becomes clearer.
—Ortega y Gasset, *Meditations on Hunting*

DEDICATION

Late February. Orion turned
the corner into the long
sleep, blindness
on the earth's black side,
as you did.
Sleet. Cloud.
Woodsmoke creeping
like a whipped dog flat
to the ground, and heaven
was all occultation.
So the few last bitter lights,
down to Betelgeuse,
in familiar constellation—
they slipped away
before I'd caught the art
of seeing, harder art
of naming. Early
fall now, now again
the wanderers —the winter
planets, memory, restless birds—
begin to shift. It will be greater
darkness if the language skulks,
unrisen.

Flesh of my flesh,
you pause to take
quick breath
against the quick descent of evening.
I feel that exhalation
along the throat, I wear you
as I wear your threaded
hunter's coat, my father.
From which in this gust
into night there climbs
—like word or star—
a single feather. . . .

Prelude

As I began I will begin with teachers, certain lusts
like theirs. Mild father. Uncle (hard). Two others—
Ray and Creston, slim and stout, tight-lipped and voluble
in order. All their hands, however, grip
firearms in mind the same. The eyes are also fire.

Behind me Father stands, his arms enfolding, as he's done
in sleep-fogged hours when I've staggered with him down
the hall to pee. His fingers steady the .22
—firm but gentle as those nights he steadies
my tiny member, yet to explode in a later rage.
If the galaxies are giants,
my own world's small at seven. Still, he urges me
to squint along the level sights, to bring that world
down further yet, to the straitest cylinder of seeing.
He never says that this will open out the landscape
in a lifetime. Tin cans plink and fly a disappointing
distance into weeds. Ducks on Swamp Creek, scarcely
ruffled, drift to recollection's edge. They will return.
So much will not be caught.
I breathe ineptitude from the still warm air.
Sumneytown, September. 1949.

Uncle brakes the jeep.
He folds his arms around himself and nods to the lane
where a cottontail is grazing, slow with August worms

and grass. I see a cloud of insects over him,
an aura. "Look right down the barrel," Uncle whispers;
dirt flies over him as the rifle cracks and cracks again.
The cartridge whinnies off a rock between us.
Stiff with age and unalarmed, he shambles into soy
my uncle farms. He jams the clutch, eyes narrowed, mutters
"down the barrel," disengages.
Ambler, 1951.

On his gun butt Creston taps a woodcock's skull. Birds
have eyes as cruel as murder. Not the woodcock, though.
The eye seems puzzled, soft as mud
in which he bores for food, and gentle. One expects a tear.
Later, soaked an hour or two in lemon, oil, and something
sweet (cranberry plucked from a bog, plain jam or honey),
he gives up his woodsfloor taste. Even the tiny bones
are edible, if you cook them as big Creston did
—squinting through the birch smoke, Grand Lake Stream,
    Maine—
split, on an outdoor fire. Creston's vision dazzles
as he reads the signs: shit, tracks, the slightest scuffing
in a feed patch. I hunt, far second best,
the country still, sometimes by naked eye alone.
Small popple by a highway, and I hear in mind the clap of
    partridge
wings, or whistle of the woodcock, as I dream that Creston
    would,
up-bursting from his worms or rest.

Snake-thin and hasty, but alert, Ray keeps
his pace uphill or down. The sight astounds
until his sockets fill with cataracts like water
in a buck's track when he's gone. He feeds,
says Ray, on the far side of the ridge he beds on
—superstition lost on Creston,

who like any hunter has his own. Like me: I spread
my decoys in a J, or rig the bird dog's bell with buckle
always to the right,and always eat red meat for breakfast,
hunting mornings. It is Vermont before the A-frames and
  chalets
have quilled our earth, but there is rarity
of game, and always was. There was before the gun,
the bow. This myth
                    it is that works us through the brakes
in fever, sidehills gone to purple as the season ends.
On days that ended with a limit, still we knew the drive
to pure annihilation. Always there was in mind
some time when birds flew up in coveys, when we chased
the singles down. Each flush gave center to the country
like a metaphor you've read and read again, and every
reading, every study, is that center
fully new and nearly fully found.
And still those coveys crowd the mind, unlimited, as ghosts
live on in dream.

In Dream: 1

Dreamer: So much has flown.
Father: Game. The mammals, birds. . . .
Dreamer: Gone on the tongue and turned to words.
Father: You think the land is going or has gone. . . .
Dreamer: It is, it has.
Father: Just as you speak, you're wrong. . . .

Instructions: The Dog *(Ray speaks)*

He's not a pet, not meant to be.
Keep him outdoors in a well-built pen, roofed over.
A roofless pen won't hold a natural hunter.
He'll look you in the eye for longer than just any
dog when you look at him. When he's a pup,
just let him go, just let him chase. You'll let him
know birds are his business. You want it so
you might as well call that birch tree as him
when he's got his nose in something. If he's smart
he'll teach himself to quarter, hunt the wind,
and slow so not to bump the birds. At last
he'll point. He has an instinct. Understand,
respect it, feel it. Don't give a lot of orders.
Be in shape. Keep up. Don't make him wait.
A bird will sit for just so long, and he
will know —if he's worth keeping— better far
than you *how* long. Be sure before you shoot
in the early months. He needs to find a thread
among the point, the flush, the shot. Dead bird.
If he wants to, let him chew the first ones up.
Get him all excited for a bird.
You'll find another. Watch the feathers burst
up in the breeze. He'll hurt the bird much less
than you imagine. Stand right still in honor
of the point from time to time: a front leg lifted,
nose a-quiver, eyes unblinking. All
that concentration of the senses! Then walk in,
excited, heart still pounding after all
the years and kills, the autumn air still tangy
to a poor man's scent, the bird in there somewhere
thinking a quick route out of sight.

And if you swing the gun too fast or slow
you will not eat. Be careful. These aren't practice rounds.
And when at last he dies, you get him quickly,
quickly as a man can make it, in the ground.

The Wrong Way Will Haunt You   (Shooting a hound)

Spittle beads as ice along
her jaw on this last winter day.
And when I lift her, all her bones
are loose and light as sprigs of hay.

For years her wail has cut the woods
in parts, familiar. Hosts of hares
have glanced behind as she ploughed on
and pushed them to me unawares.

Now her muzzle skims the earth
as if she breathed a far dim scent,
and yet she holds her tracks to suit
my final, difficult intent.

For years with gun in hand I sensed
her circle shrinking to my point.
How odd that ever I should be
the center to that whirling hunt.

Here a yip and there a chop
meant some prime buck still blessed with breath,
and in the silences I feared
she'd run him to her own cold death.

The snow that clouds my sights could be
a trailing snow, just wet and new
enough to keep a scent alive,
but not so deep that she'd fall through.

She falls without a sound. Her blood
runs circular upon the ground.
I lug her to those thick strange woods
where she put our first hare around.

I kick a drift-top over her
(the hardpan won't accept my spade).
The wind makes up a howl as in
all cold old ballads on The Grave.

In Dream: 2   (Grooming the woods)

The sidehill where the old burn was, and berries
for the birds and bears on sabered vines, through which
the rodents tunneled, counting on the cover
from nightfowl, prowlers —I
could go there, hearing things, at night in moon
or dark of moon. The black-scorched soil
pushed up rough clumps of gray birch, sumac, cabbage
pine. The sidehill in the dream is cleared
to lawn. There is some trouble in the air,
I don't at first know what. I stand far off,
high up, on Bailey's Ridge, my eyes aren't good
enough to see across the valley. Then,
somehow I'm brought up close. And now I see
the well-groomed hordes of new-age mountain "farmers"

in the bordering woods. *They're painting all the trees!*
They've cut the weed brush down, the feed —the popple,
choking alder, maple suckers. Painting
on the bigger boles! I know they think they're adding
Beauty. Something in the dream informs me.
Tasteful ochers, purples (solemn ones), and burnt
siennas. . . . My tongue is straining at my teeth,
but I can't speak. They're all for Nature. Helpers.
Come closer still, I find the stripes they paint
conform into directionals: "The Ledge—
One Mile This Way"; "The Waterfall—Turn Right";
"Where We Once Saw a Deer Track—Just Ahead";
et cetera. My bedclothes are a wilderness.

Instructions: Locating Yourself   (Creston speaks)

Without some superstition any bigwoods is a puzzle,
mystery. So's the sky, a lake, all out-of-doors.
That's why I've taught you how to fix the decoys in that J,
that's why I tell you to believe that old decaying lumber
ramps along a grown-up tote-road point to water,
that's why you must believe no book
is worth a damn out here, and must believe
the line-gales of the autumn plow the lake in windrows—
and foam can tell you where you are. And who and why.
Just read the signs. Even tracks so fresh they're filling up
right while you look are ghosts. They're partly superstition.
Mine are. Watch me disappear one day. We've made
a lot of tracks together. If you can't see them once
I'm in the ground, the woods will jumble, you'll be lost.
For good.
                    (He sinks back in)

The "organic" husbandman with cheek of tan
for my hunting hates me. And I him. He'll be a friend
to all the animals and birds.
Pheasants are ground-feeding fowl.
They'd love the millet that he spills
in harvesting for bread. But snow up here's too deep
for pheasants to break through to eat.
The winter kills them. They'd add beauty,
so his sign's designed
to shield his "pheasants" from me, others like me.
And the husbandman has put a cattle lick down in
his "pasture" for the bucks and does. For salt.
Not even his pathetic cows eat salt
in winter, and it's now the hard bare end
of January. So sitting by his antique woodstove,
he won't see his deer. Alackaday!
The redneck hunters, he believes,
destroy them all!
And all the gorgeous pheasants, too. From China.

Partridge are our native bird.
I see them for a second in dead winter, flashing
out of treetops where they bud. If times are hard,
they'll chew on hemlock tips like deer. I shot one
out of season once, on a slow day's rabbit hunt. He tasted
like the hemlock tree itself. And speak about "organic"!
The bird becomes his feed: in autumn, filled with fruit
from vine or thorn, his craw's a case of jewels;
he'll crop the popple bud in any season,
if our new-style "farmers" let the saplings thrive.

But they are bent on better things —which means to clearing
all they can, all flavor of experience.

My own at least: the muted, layered feathers
puffed from grouse to hang in air
—more beautiful than pheasants' gaudy wear—
then vanish into woods like all the fathers.

A dead bird's eye seems placidly to ponder
everything that I can't know: the past,
the history that joined us both at last,
joy and woe commingling. That's the wonder —

for every living bird there is a man.
In every slaughtered bird are many men.
Word. Father. Taste on the tongue. Friend.
Explain this to the husbandman, the cow
lover, sign painter. How the feathers blow!
The buried dogs, the meanings, men.

Crow-Killing in the Eisenhower Years. Fourth Month (1953)

Braving the columns
of fog, the dark,
Sam and I staggered
an hour before dawn
to our blind underneath
the big twin gums,
past stamping hooves
in wet turf, huffed breath,
and the double dim fires
of late spring night
farm animals' stares.
It was as it is
a matter of keeping
an edge on the foe,
and the war was something
we learned as we fought.
We hated each crow,
since each was evil,
each would thieve
from the very devil,
who might —awakened
by gunfire at daybreak—
have been my uncle.

The campaign was modest
at the start —an owl

of dew-rotted pasteboard,
two paper decoys,
a plastic call—
but we scuffed our boots
over clump and furrow
like the tough town dagos
on the streets by the mill
(Weymouth Asbestos)
in jackets whose silk
glittered maps of Korea.
Reno, Butch, and
(unaccountably) "Dutch."
We salted our talk
with commies and chinks,
how we'd blow them to hell,
though the years kill more
than we ever killed:
Reno went nuts;
Dutch married badly;
Butch died of drink
on the seat of a Ford.
A dentist transformed
the ghost-hallowed barn
on the neighbors' farm
to an office. As clever
as only the wicked
know how to be clever,
the outlaws escaped us
each morning till Sam
(before he discovered
the girls) bought a hawk
at an old-style auction
for a tough old buck.
Wings spread, he was fierce

in death, and noble
as the mother country's
unflappable eagle,
and we made progress
at last! Battalions
of crows —gone crazy
to strafe him— blackened
the sky, or clung
—strange ebony apples—
to our shelter trees.

Commandos! We beat back the dark enemies.

Coon Hunt. Sixth Month (1955)

By late in spring the cottonmouths and rattlers
began to move. You didn't dare use dogs.
Sam Spurley eased the flatbed truck along
the red-dirt lanes, and Purdy sang out loud:
"Hey FROG! Hey CRIP! Hey Billy-BEAN!"
And true to every witless white cliché
the black men loped from their cabins, every stop,
visible only by teeth and eyes. And I
and my two brothers would blush, embarrassed, shamed,
when Purdy, playing his light among the cypress,
hooted "Thar one!" And we three couldn't
see him for our lives, and all the blacks
would shake with laughter: "What? You white boys *blind?*"
And we would have to hand our shotgun over
to one of them, who would tumble the coon to ground.

There came a night when we heard the bawl of hounds
in spite of snakes, just as we saw the cruiser
—GEORGIA STATE POLICE in black along
the front-door panels—and a light switched on.
A fat cop pulled a gun and bellowed, "What
the fuck you niggers doin' here?" Then saw
us three, as pale as possum kits. And one
of us spoke up, "We're just out hunting coons."
And laughing, he: "Hot damn, son! So are we. . . ."
And told us all we'd best be headed now,
because the handlers, cussing through the swamp,
might hear our shots and think they had their man.
"Not if you wasn't plannin' to shoot him they won't,"
sang Purdy, bolder than hell, if only we knew it.
The cracker trained the light on his eyes, so blinding

bright that even Purdy couldn't see through it.

Sin and Fear. Eighth Month (1957)

A slate-color heron stood as the ground fog cleared and
    changed
to soup of August. No motion. Even the salamanders
the heron stabbed each morning settled into mud
so still the great bird's pondering eye could not detect them.
That wicked eye appeared —impossibly!— to droop.
The ducks of Swamp Creek, moulting now, began to hop
frog-awkward, flightless, out of wilted pickerelweed.
We crouched in a blind on shore.
We were all but naked, dressed in swimming trunks to be
our own retrievers. Just beyond point-blank,

we'd blow the grainy mallards' heads off, pluck and cook them
in the evening cool. We waited for the ducks to school
so as to slaughter more than one with every shot,
and huddled in that quick-breathed waiting close as lovers.
A lifeless breeze cuffed at the pond, cattail, weed.
We saw it riffle dingy feathers. But it carried, too,
somehow a smell of suppurating carcass, harsh
and dreary all at once. It seemed at least to me
the stench the soul must make in wrenching free
of the body, to flap along the suffocating lonely
ages into the Hell they talked about on Sunday.
Uphill behind us
out of sight, there was the sound of labored breathing,
or was it wings? Across the swamps and fields just then
there came the awful howling of my uncle's hunting dogs,
unlikely energetic in such a torpid dawn,
and way off in the shimmering pasture horses reared
and whinnied, bolting headlong in spite of summer bellies.
The ducks left the brook a lather, kicking for absolute center
of the gray-brown slue. Then all was quiet again.
We skulked in terror homeward, Charlie, Michael, I —
two dead now, twenty years gone by. I can't explain
that fear, the way our tears sprang up! Then dried.

The Brink of the Season: Ninth Month

Joey and I on the river,
where it bends sharp west near the falls.
September, but it's still summer —

one of the few remaining
bluebird days. An osprey,
one of the few remaining,

poised in backlight, screams
from an elm. A black-crowned heron,
such as I haven't seen

in years, has speared a frog.
O, the predators!
In a week we'll be among them,

shotguns bursting the still
as now a black bass bursts
the glaze of water to kill

a yellow butterfly
who waited excusably long
to make his astonishing way

to Mexico: why leave now?
For cornflowers hold to the banks,
and only alarmist crowds

of maple scrub depart
from familiar green —deluding
shade of summer. Our art

—scouting for ducks— is soft
as the very season. Canoe-quiet,
we ride an invisible waft

of breeze far into the slue.
Like boats themselves, shed feathers,
hopeful signs, ride too:

small escorts on either side,
they are not more silent than we.
I watch a sweat drop slide

down the back of Joey's neck.
I can dream I hear it, and then
I hear the ludicrous cluck

ahead of mallards at feed.
And the pitiable call of wood duck
up in the winter-rye seed.

Joe turns in the seat, his hunter's
grin is hungry, wide
and wild. He is my mirror,

I am suddenly sure; and sudden
also, within the calm,
the distaste I feel for our mission.

I should cry to the ducks: "Get out!"
or some such harmless phrase.
I want to upset the boat,

and every duck to jump.
I'd permit them their awkwardness,
scudding the surface. They'd pump

across the unsmirched sheet
of sky. Let the heavy mallards
chuckle, the wood duck squeak

at *us*, then the river revert
to silence. But I don't cry out.
I wait for more loaded words,

by design or perforce. I can't tell
what appetite brings me here,
nor what is the part of will

in repeating what one has long done.
For months a plan has been set.
We imitate long guns,

clap paddles against the thwarts
till ducks seem to scrawl the air,
then are gone. But though they depart,

some will return to fall
—dark meat of roasted wood duck,
blood-red of mallard broiled;

the weather will break, and, broken,
the spurious summer limp off.
I will speak. I will have spoken.

I know Joey's heart like mine
is fluttering here in the boat,
the canoe of fading green

that seems like an insect to hover
over the sheen of the water.
The words are poised in the throat.

Early Season: Tenth Month (1958, 1978)

An early chill in October. Geese
announce themselves, their cries are pain,
invite it. This is clarity of fall
perhaps, the heart is sick for wonder and with wonder.

In 1958, the nut trees shed
reluctantly their leaves. Click
of the brown oak, muslin beech
in the gusts. We slipped among spilled acorns.

His yellowed eyes were more like hazelnuts. Elwood's
face lay black as shadow against
the frosted trunks he lay his cheek on, sighting
up. The crown-boughs towered so high

I felt myself an awkward spy
in another forbidden dimension.
And when at last the squirrel betrayed himself
at the top, he seemed immense.

It was a time when, full of pain
beyond my own defining, I
would sit and stare. Miraculous TV!
Behold a wonder! Circus girls in tights,

the rose-lipped singers of *Your Hit Parade!*
Through damnable keyholes I spied on the maid.
Or raced my aging half-bred mare
through winter wheat, screaming.

The neighbors' bookworm daughter Marcia
read by her attic window. I stood,
knees shaking in the shifting straw
of pinewoods by her father's cattle shed.

I craned my neck and clawed the branches,
muttering, jumping when the pony snorted.
The Princess in the Tower!
                              Elwood shot.
Time tumbled, tumbled on

and down. I shot into my first
young woman. Pain
somehow, and diminution,
just as the squirrel seemed somehow smaller

lying underfoot among the leaves.
With age all women climb to mystery
again, and geese are calling from that high dimension,
as fall clears out a way for the white of winter.

Late Season: Eleventh Month   *(Ray confronts the new "farmer")*

"Didn't see your sign."
                    "I guess you're blind?"
"Blinder than I choose. It's cataracts. . . .
I've hunted here these years, and never planned
someone would stop me. I've made a lot of tracks
along this edge: there's decent bottomland
for woodcock, and thorn up on the ridges —partridge
like that stuff. . . ."
                    "I don't want a cartridge
in my milking goats."
(Goats? Sweet Jesus!)
"You won't get a cartridge.
You won't get a thing, Lord knows,
but fine shot's all *I* use for birding. . . .BB's?"
(There must, Ray thinks, be some way I can reason
with him, keep him happy. When it snows,
I'll hike in from the other side. Deer season:
that's what I'm up to, scouting out the signs;
why else does he think
I'd come without a dog to walk his ground?
But what the hell does *he* know? Damn his kind
to that same hell. They'd make my old aunts drink.
This one here, I've seen him at the town
meeting, with his friends, in coveralls
and holding peaveys, dung forks, roofing tools,
to show us, like their signs, they're farmers now.
I'd like to get one at the other end
of a saw, or watch one trail a plow. . . .)

"You're in here hunting? And you're
                    half blind?
It's bad enough you kill off all the game,
but worse that you're a killer who can't see.
You'd better go."

"I see the game all right. By ear. In mind.
I know which way they go
by now. Come over by that little tree. . . ."
                    "I've meant to cut that. . . ."
"Sure. But just the same,
come over here a minute. Can you see?"
                    "See what?"
"See where a horny buck has thrashed
it all to hell. No, on the other side. . . ."
                    "I hadn't noticed."
"Well, I'm not surprised."
                    "Now don't be smart."
"Can't help it. Smart's a thing I learned to be;
you better learn when you're brought up short of cash.
And smart means chasing down a thing worth eating. . . ."
                    "Well, never mind. . . .
I plan to keep the wildlife wild. And free."

"You just keep clearing back the brush, the vines —
you won't have too much wildlife to be keeping."

All day revolving wind and snow. Now whirligigs
with evening —flake, blown feather, leaf—
alight, though memory and want in eddies
live, stay on, and will forever. Deep
inside the game I feed my children lies
the tracery of nerve and bone and muscle
that impelled the birds to spiral. Deep within
my vulgar bloom of paunch, the leanness of
my son who flies, it seems, with every bite
to manhood. And the frail conspiracy
of beauties in my roly daughter hints
itself, her flesh as clear as fifth-month tadpoles',
all that pulsing mechanism made
near visible in kitchen light, while out
of doors the darkness lowers toward cold ground.
The meadow fence turns monolithic, black
on the horizontal. Meadow, where the fluff
of springtime-trembling dandelions would poise.
One saw the tenuous grip of stem and slip.
From his pine again the dusk owl paddles east.
(*Great Horned* he's called, though scarcely bigger than
a dove within his cumulus of down.)
I can tell him by his profile in the backlight
as I tell the wood duck from the widgeon, small
hooded merganser from the teal by silhouette.
They circle year on year in autumn dawns.
I finish early. While the children go
on feeding, I take up my window-station,
note the falling mercury, and how
all the ridges vanish, losing contour.
Up the hill a hundred yards a stump

takes on the look of a Nimrod, tired but flush.
I fill this outline in, with the crucial
compound history of hunters —laughter,
love, and melancholy once embodied
in our lives together. And is still. Flesh of my flesh.

The sky at night is like a big city
where beasts and men abound,
but never once has anyone
killed a fowl or goat,
and no bear ever killed a prey.
There are no accidents. There are no losses.
Everything knows its way.

—Ewe Song (Africa)

Pensive Blindness: With, but Not Of Them

Even in his truck and drunk
and out of season, Creston
always threw a glance
back up the brushy twitch roads
as he passed. Those eyes!
No track along the highway
missed their notice, yet
no high hushed bird —no hawk,
no eagle— glided over
that his face did not jerk skyward,
even if death itself

(a logger's sixteen-wheeler)
shook the road ahead.
Ray, and Frank MacArthur,
Earl . . . all the same.
And those last few Indians, dead
by now —the Sopiels,
The Tomahs, Socabesins.

From them this dedication
to the sign: the orange mass
of chips the woodpeckers leave
at my feet, an unsprung alder
where some autumn buck has rubbed
his velvet off, the slick
and nauseous mound of mud
and stick where beavers lay
their musk self-advertisement,
slantwise cuts on shoots
of puckerbrush that show
a ghost-white hare in mind
in rearing human stance,
the nightfowls' outlines and
their strangely comic calls.
Still I turn my eyes
more in than out, outdoors,
must ever make myself
do otherwise —self-caught
like a conscience-burdened schoolchild
longing to attend
in church the fathers' lessons.
History's a thing
for me that seems to climb
away from track or sign
or, oftener, glances over them

to hang tree-high.
Feet touch the ground and lungs
draw in the sky, but heart
and brain are set upon
some other thing. I picture
these gone elders kneeling
near a hoofprint, dung clump, pawing,
feather, swatch of hair.
They bend to many facts
from which they reconstruct
a past that stretches back
through closed-in woods, along
the rivers, lakeshores, brooks,
the ridges, slues, and trails.
They prophesy a future,
rising from their crouches
wordless, cradling firearms.
Their eyes are bright and sure.
Still it's the elders kneeling
at last, and not their study,
that come to consciousness
among the peckings, rubbings,
cuffings behind my house.
Their ample women, too. . . .
They laugh at my inclination
to wonder. They're at home
with the way the mystery
of moving flesh will leave

its traces everywhere —
beast, bird, or baby
come to consciousness
without such constant striving,
the habit of excess.

Old Dog, New Dog

With the stylish young brood bitch, the old dog showed
the way sex still explodes
like a double barrel into the blanking winter
of a life. His ears were blanks, his eyes —
those snowy bays of cataracts. His nose
remained, and the gleaming pinkish member.
They locked, the high-blood nervous white-and-liver
dam and he. He couldn't hear his howls ·
that shook the kennel roof and shocked her
there beneath him.   Ground, rain-soaked
with spring, gave to my spade and in I rolled
his carcass, quick, still loose in body, loose
again as when he ranged this ground a puppy,
stiffened. Whirr. A shot. Dead bird. The first.
I winced as the clots fell in on him.
Pain. And nerves when the shovel clanked on rock.
The new-age mountain farmer neighbor wouldn't
understand this rite. He bought the farm
and on the trunk of every tree he hung
his signs: NO HUNTING-FISHING-TRESPASSING.
Face wet with weather, sweat, and another thing,
I shouldered my tool, but swung it once across
the almost casual path in air of a woodcock
unalarmed in June.
                    The pup I saved
is in the old dog's run. He squalls. I chose him
by his chest and length of leg, proportion
of white to orange markings (so I could see
him locked on point in brush or choking alder),
by the brightness in his eye. By superstition.
Released, he flushes hosts of starlings, grackles

from the meadow into hardhack whips and popple.
They spend their music rashly, shrill and apt.
Slow as dream, bright moths spin through the haze.
There is the sound of waters everywhere.
A grouse chick rises bee-like, barely airborne.
The dog for a moment stiffens. Then he bolts
as all the brood erupts. I let him go
for now, for birds will be his business. The hen
sits longer than the rest, then clatters out
the other way. And fooled, he chases, nose erect,
ears cocked, eyes wide, while I
—out of shape with summer, heart a hammer—
pursue downhill, half blind with my own laughter.

The Lesson: August, 1979

Four months ago my son and I broadcast our seeds of pumpkin.
The ripening fruit are ranged before us by the drought-starved
    brook,
their color that faint orange and red of maple suckers hinting
the gold to come. Already the faint whiff of apple in air,
that also bears a far complaint of early geese. Each globe
has made a target, disturbing in its semblance to a face.
I stand behind the boy and help to balance the rifle, feeling
the sun and blood of him in his cheek. He strives to line the
    distant
front sight and the near post. The barrel waves like a sapling,
the cartridge snaps. He whoops as it finds its way into the pulp
of the first great squash. Another shot, another and another.
All fly home. At last he shoots the bolt. He tells me how

he's learned to find the mark: it has to do with squeezing the
  trigger
between one beat of the heart and the next, between the sixth
  and seventh
beats from the time he raises to aim. I check myself, for I
feel an impulse to explain how game can't be expected
to wait on his magic method. For it will wait in time on
  another.
His eyes are the blue of mine, though keener. The lesson is his
  own.
Some thing in the air. First gust. The first fall leaf scales
  down.

Bellatrix Visible: Orion in the East, October

After the long long sleep, the blindness,
the Hunter climbs again, returning
from the journey east, where rays of sun
fell on his eyes, as the story goes,   The Wanderer.
We fall to eating. The first feast —
the ducks that dipped to my decoys, rigged
in their meaningful J, the grouse that froze
before the staunch young pointer. Doe-eyed woodcock.
Surrounded by family. It is this blood
that turns on the tongue to words, and the land
rises again in mind like a planet,
its contours of fear   lust   sin   and love,
that mixed topography of the heart,
dark meat composed of earth and air.
The spirit tinkles like a collar bell,
between tears and triumph. There is a subject outside
the self that engages more than the self.

I gnaw a bone till it's gleaming clean
as any star in a constellation
that hangs on a world which invites us still to dwell,
within it, where blood is still a consolation.

Bellatrix, like a gorgeous wound in the arch. . . .

The New Year: 1980

Father. Uncle. Ray. Frank, George and Creston MacArthur.
Earl Bonness. Bill Fitch. Carter White. Purdy Gibbons.
Joey Olsen. Hazen Bagley. Clay Bartlett. Terry Lawson.
David Tobey. Lola Socabesin. Leo Sopiel. David Tomah.
Sam Spurley. Bill White. Elwood Johnson. I breathe
the aptitude of names. The ducks are flown. They will return.
The deer are yarded. The grouse take shelter under brittle
    crust.
The crows patrol the frozen tote-roads. Squirrels huddle
    in holes.
The she-bear snuffs in unimaginable dream, a month till her
    term.
Those apt old places freeze in mind: The Hedgehog Den, The
    Lake
of One Mistake, Slewgundy Ridge, Hardscrabble, Quintown,
    Eagle,
Sweet Marie Cove, The Thousand-Acre Burn, Camilla's
    Heartbreak.
Oak smoke from my chimney straight as a thread among
    a sign,
a raising of game, a shot, a search, a find, a shout, a feast.

Ten o'clock. The familiar constellation just off south.
Moon and stars and planets fall into frost on branch and brush
that wink in the influence, every node of light a name or face
or place that's lit like a bird. For a moment I know what
the saved must feel,
as I whistle my dogs up, kick uphill,
through the light of heavenly fields.

History Is Your Own Heartbeat
Michael S. Harper (1971)

The Foreclosure
Richard Emil Braun (1972)

The Scrawny Sonnets and
Other Narratives
Robert Bagg (1973)

The Creation Frame
Phyllis Thompson (1973)

To All Appearances: Poems New
and Selected
Josephine Miles (1974)

Nightmare Begins Responsibility
Michael S. Harper (1975)

The Black Hawk Songs
Michael Borich (1975)

The Wichita Poems
Michael Van Walleghen (1975)

Cumberland Station
Dave Smith (1977)

Tracking
Virginia R. Terris (1977)

Poems of the Two Worlds
Frederick Morgan (1977)

Images of Kin: New and
Selected Poems
Michael S. Harper (1977)

On Earth as It Is
Dan Masterson (1978)

Riversongs
Michael Anania (1978)

Goshawk, Antelope
Dave Smith (1979)

Death Mother and Other Poems
Frederick Morgan (1979)

Local Men
James Whitehead (1979)

Coming to Terms
Josephine Miles (1979)

Searching the Drowned Man
Sydney Lea (1980)

With Akhmatova at the
Black Gates
Stephen Berg (1981)

More Trouble with the Obvious
Michael Van Walleghen (1981)

Dream Flights
Dave Smith (1981)

The American Book of the Dead
Jim Barnes (1982)

Northbook
Frederick Morgan (1982)

The Floating Candles
Sydney Lea (1982)